THE RAILROAD
IN AMERICAN HISTORY

ELECTRIC
TRAINS
AND
TROLLEYS
(1880–PRESENT)

John Bankston

Mitchell Lane
PUBLISHERS

P.O. Box 196
Hockessin, Delaware 19707

THE RAILROAD
IN AMERICAN HISTORY

The Birth of the Locomotive
The Railroad Comes to America
The Railroad Grows into an Industry
The Railroad and the Civil War
The Railroad Fuels Westward Expansion
Electric Trains and Trolleys

The publisher would like to thank Milton C. Hallberg for acting as a consultant on its *The Railroad in American History* series. He is a professor emeritus of agricultural economics at Pennsylvania State University and has been a visiting professor at universities around the world. His railroad interests began when he attended a railroad telegraphers' school in preparation for a job as a depot agent on the CB&Q Railroad in Illinois. After retiring from teaching, he returned to his railroad interests as a new hobby, during which time he has written about early rail systems.

PUBLISHER'S NOTE:
The facts on which this book is based have been thoroughly researched. Documentation of such research can be found on page 44. While every possible effort has been made to ensure accuracy, the publisher will not assume liability for damages caused by inaccuracies in the data, and makes no warranty on the accuracy of the information contained herein.

Printing
1   2   3   4   5   6   7   8   9

Library of Congress Cataloging-in-Publication Data
Bankston, John, 1974-
Electric trains and trolleys (1880-1920) / by John Bankston.
    p. cm. —(The railroad in American history)
Includes bibliographical references and index.
ISBN 978-1-61228-291-6 (library bound)
1. Electric railroads--History—Juvenile literature. 2.—Electric railroads—United States--History—Juvenile literature. 3. Street-railroads—United States—History—Juvenile literature. I. Title.
TF856.B36 2013
385.0973'09034—dc23
                                                    2012009416

eBook ISBN: 9781612283654

PLB

CONTENTS

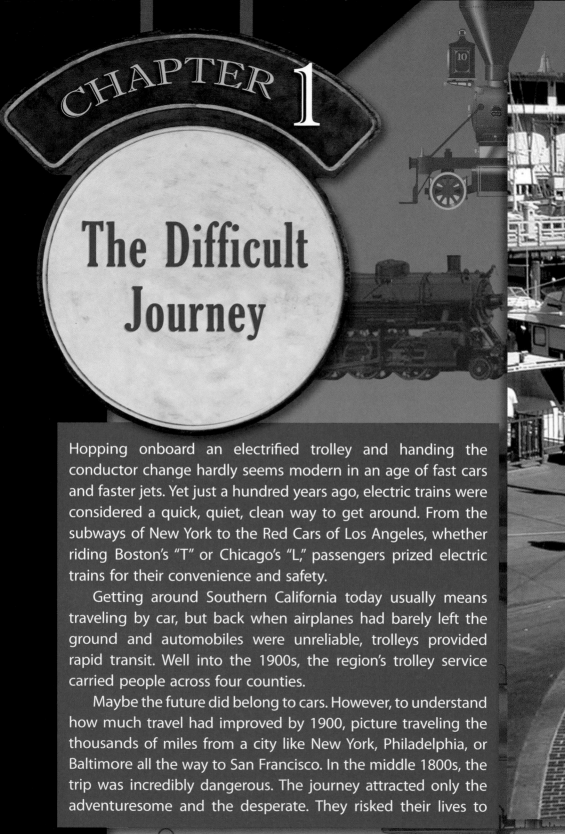

CHAPTER 1

The Difficult Journey

Hopping onboard an electrified trolley and handing the conductor change hardly seems modern in an age of fast cars and faster jets. Yet just a hundred years ago, electric trains were considered a quick, quiet, clean way to get around. From the subways of New York to the Red Cars of Los Angeles, whether riding Boston's "T" or Chicago's "L," passengers prized electric trains for their convenience and safety.

Getting around Southern California today usually means traveling by car, but back when airplanes had barely left the ground and automobiles were unreliable, trolleys provided rapid transit. Well into the 1900s, the region's trolley service carried people across four counties.

Maybe the future did belong to cars. However, to understand how much travel had improved by 1900, picture traveling the thousands of miles from a city like New York, Philadelphia, or Baltimore all the way to San Francisco. In the middle 1800s, the trip was incredibly dangerous. The journey attracted only the adventuresome and the desperate. They risked their lives to

Trolleys continue to run in cities like San Francisco

pursue dreams of fortune while escaping uncertain pasts. They were mainly adult men, but some women and children also made the journey.

Loading their luggage onto a steamboat in New York, western-bound travelers headed south toward the Florida Keys at about ten miles (sixteen kilometers) per day. Crossing the island chain they pushed into the Gulf of Mexico before making landfall at the port of Aspinwall, Panama.

It would have been a long, chaotic voyage. Ships were often lost at sea—done in by bad weather, bad piloting, or bad luck. Steerage passengers who could only afford the cheapest tickets were locked in a large room below deck where they were plagued by poor meals and diseases.

The most dangerous part, however, was crossing the Isthmus of Panama. Before 1855, when a railroad was finally completed across the

Completed in 1855, the railroad crossing the Isthmus of Panama was literally a lifesaver. It made the fifty-mile (eighty-kilometer) journey much easier for travelers.

isthmus, the fifty-mile (eighty-kilometer) trek was made on foot or on horseback, assisted by pack mules. Thieves and cholera stalked the travelers. By 1850, unmarked graves were all that was left of the hundreds who never reached the Pacific Ocean. In 1852, the future commander of Union forces during the Civil War, Ulysses S. Grant, led a regiment of 600 soldiers across Panama. More than one hundred people died before they reached Panama City, where they boarded another ship bound for California.

Avoiding this trip meant crossing the United States by land. This was even riskier. In May 1846, the ill-fated Donner Party—bound for California from Missouri––wound up snowbound in the Sierra Nevada Mountains. They would not be rescued until February of the next year. By then only forty-eight of the original eighty-seven survived. The tragedy became well known partly because many survivors had resorted to cannibalism. They ate the dead.

Even without tragic outcomes, horse-and-wagon trips across the country were long and uncomfortable. Despite the obstacles, in 1865, easterners were being urged by leaders of the day to go west. Many listened.

By 1869, the transcontinental railroad line linked San Francisco to New York. Tracks crisscrossed North America. Anyone with the money (tickets for the trip could be over one hundred dollars at a time when many earned just two dollars a day) could travel by rail. By the 1880s, a train trip from New York to San Francisco could be made in less than a week.

The East was settled by men with horses. They rode them or used them to pull coaches and carriages. The West was settled by people who rode the rails. No longer were trips limited to the hardy and the foolish, the brave and the reckless. The safety and comfort of the rails meant that many more people were willing to make the trip. Because the trip was no longer risky, men brought along their wives and children. A few single women even made the trip.

Able to speed up or brake quickly, electrically powered interurban trolleys like the one shown here greatly expanded both the distances people could travel and the cities in which they were located.

The countryside was transformed by steam-powered trains. The cities, however, were changed by electrically powered trains and trolleys. New York and Chicago expanded outward when trolleys and electric trains sped commuters from jobs in the city to homes in distant suburbs. Nowhere was the trolley's influence more dramatic, however, than in Southern California.

Sometimes called the interurban (because it connected cities and towns), the electrically powered trolley's "influence was greatest in creating the city of Southern California," author Spencer Crump says, describing the huge urban region stretching from San Diego to just north of Los Angeles. "In other regions of America, the interurbans came after the areas had been settled generally and they did little more than supplement development. In Southern California the interurban was the pioneer. After its arrival the population followed."[1]

Trolleys helped create sprawling urban areas like the ones in Southern California. Today people living in four different counties travel back and forth to work in Los Angeles, sometimes spending more than three hours a day in their cars. In the beginning, however electric trains were the answer to getting from place to place.

Fans of Travel

Beach's subway

Inventors in the 1800s imagined all kinds of ways to move groups of people rapidly from one place to another. They considered hot air balloons and underground horse-drawn carriages. They even explored the idea of moving sidewalks—much like the ones inside of modern airports. Few ideas were as unusual as the one explored by inventor Alfred Ely Beach. He wanted to use a giant fan to move people. He didn't just dream it. He built it.

Beach was the son of a cabinetmaker and the nephew of Benjamin H. Day, founder of *The Sun,* a major New York City newspaper. He was also owner of *Scientific American,* a magazine founded in 1845 that people still read today. Beach invented an early version of the typewriter and a later model designed for the blind. In 1865, he invented the pneumatic tube.

It used compressed air to push an object through a tube. Long before email was invented, containers carrying messages zoomed through tubes in offices. They are still used by drive-up customers at banks.

Unable to get approval from New York City officials, Beach began constructing his subway tunnel in secret. On February 28, 1870, Beach's subway opened. Operating a single car with room for twenty-two people, the subway was propelled by a large fan. It traveled only a single block, starting at City Hall and running under a busy stretch of Broadway. During its first year, some 400,000 people paid a quarter for a ride. Although Beach ran out of money, his experiment proved that New Yorkers would pay to ride underground.

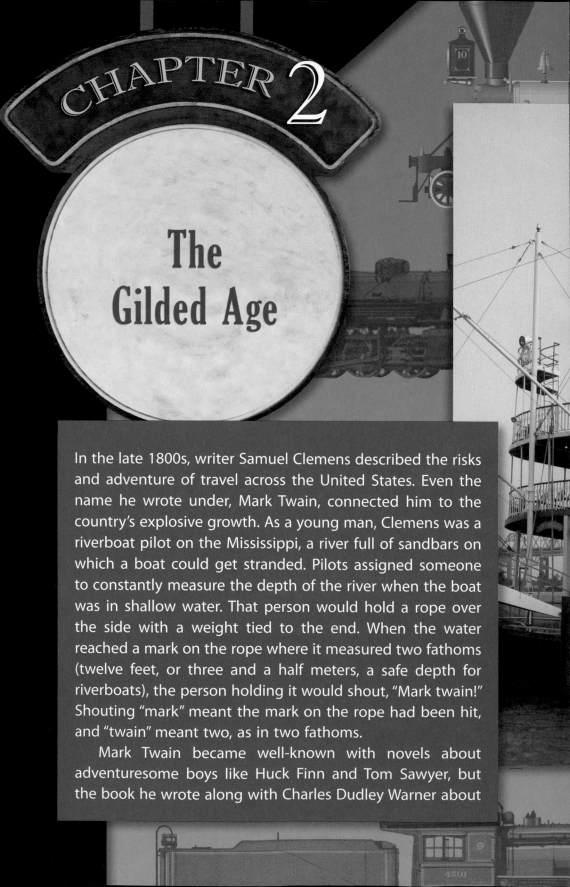

CHAPTER 2

The Gilded Age

In the late 1800s, writer Samuel Clemens described the risks and adventure of travel across the United States. Even the name he wrote under, Mark Twain, connected him to the country's explosive growth. As a young man, Clemens was a riverboat pilot on the Mississippi, a river full of sandbars on which a boat could get stranded. Pilots assigned someone to constantly measure the depth of the river when the boat was in shallow water. That person would hold a rope over the side with a weight tied to the end. When the water reached a mark on the rope where it measured two fathoms (twelve feet, or three and a half meters, a safe depth for riverboats), the person holding it would shout, "Mark twain!" Shouting "mark" meant the mark on the rope had been hit, and "twain" meant two, as in two fathoms.

Mark Twain became well-known with novels about adventuresome boys like Huck Finn and Tom Sawyer, but the book he wrote along with Charles Dudley Warner about

The *Natchez* is one of only six true steam-powered steamboats on the Mississippi today.

Mark Twain on the right shakes the hand of actor John T. Raymond, who starred as Colonel Sellers in the stage production of *The Gilded Age*.

adults growing rich in the late nineteenth century gave a name to the era. It was called *The Gilded Age: A Tale of Today.*

The Gilded Age was, explains historian Les Standiford " . . . a period that stretched from the end of the Civil War until the Great Crash of 1929, marked by unbounded industrial growth and prosperity, and an optimism that was barely dimmed by World War I." Twain's book was fairly negative toward the growth of the country and the enormous fortunes some made as a result, however, Standiford says, "public confidence and personal wealth was growing at an unprecedented rate."[1]

Colonel Beriah Sellers, the main character in *The Gilded Age,* was forever trying get-rich-quick schemes and failing miserably. "The Colonel's tongue was a magician's wand," Twain wrote, "that turned dried apples into figs and water into wine as easily as it could change a hovel into a palace and present poverty into future riches." [2]

In the United States a penniless immigrant named Joseph Pulitzer became wealthy as a newspaper publisher. Inventors like Alexander Graham Bell and Thomas Alva Edison matched Pulitzer's riches by creating devices that improved millions of American lives. It's no wonder that in the 1890s, Dr. Russell H. Conwell pointed out, "I say you ought to be rich; you have no right to be poor." [3]

In 1869, the transcontinental railroad was completed; seven years later Bell invented the telephone. Trains and telephones were ideal for a country where the eastern boundary was some 3,000 miles (4,800 kilometers) from the west. One invention allowed people to travel across the country; the other allowed them to talk about it.

The Gilded Age was a period of rapid change. "By the 1880s," explains historian Charles W. Calhoun, "homes and offices were illuminated by electric lamps, factory production lines were driven by electric motors and urban commuters clamored aboard electric trolleys."[4]

People no longer had to live close to where they worked. In the beginning of the 1800s, most city dwellers walked from home to job.

By the middle of the century, they might have taken a streetcar (also called a trolley) pulled by horses or a steam engine. Because it could accelerate and brake quickly, the electric trolley became the perfect vehicle for city commutes with frequent stops. Soon it was possible to live many miles from where one worked—giving birth to the suburbs.

"Streetcars, which played the largest role in creating workers' suburbs, did so in two typical ways," explains Thomas J. Schlereth in his book *Victorian America.* Schlereth writes, "Car lines might be laid out to existing hamlets [towns] . . . or car tracks might run through undeveloped land (often owned by railway executives) to create new residential communities."[5]

New sources of power altered lives. When factories relied on water to power their equipment, they had to be built near rivers or other waterways. The steam engine allowed factories to be built just about anywhere. Factory workers lived close to their jobs—often in overpriced, rundown apartments. Most owners and managers did not want to live

Electric trains would even be able to offer scenic routes along mountainsides

near factories, which were generally noisy and produced horrible-smelling fumes. While horse-drawn carriages and trolleys carried these early commuters, it took the efforts of a German engineer who first did his research in prison to help move industry and transportation away from steam.

Werner von Siemens was one of fourteen children born to a poor farmer. Unable to afford college, he joined the military and learned the fundamentals of engineering. Besides researching gold and silver plating in a prison laboratory (he served time for dueling), Siemens constructed a pointer telegraph in 1847 improving the era's primary means of communication. It used real letters instead of Morse code. It was the "dynamo-electric machine" he invented in 1866, however, which had the greatest impact on transportation.

The dynamo-electric principle was an important step in using electricity to power trains. Before its discovery, electric power could only be obtained through batteries, which quickly ran down. Siemens's

The Siemens Electric Railway appeared at an 1879 exhibition and carried passengers on three carriages.

dynamo was a generator that converted mechanical energy into electrical energy in an economical way.

His work led to the first electrically powered streetlights—installed in Berlin in 1879. That same year he demonstrated the first electric railway. Two years later, the world's first electric streetcar began operating in Germany.

An electric locomotive usually gets its power in one of three ways: from overhead electrical lines, from an electrified "third rail" set beside the standard two, or from an onboard storage device such as a battery.

One of the advantages of electrically powered trains is they can be powered by distant fuel sources. Instead of carrying coal or diesel fuel, an electric train can receive electricity from a water-powered hydroelectric plant or a nuclear power plant. Someday even wind-powered or solar-powered plants could supply the energy for an electric train.

Even when the power plant uses coal or oil, using electricity to power a train is cleaner and faster. Unfortunately, it is also more expensive. This is why electric trains in the United States are mostly limited to densely populated areas. Powering every cross-country train by electric lines would be too costly. Still, the power that has fueled transportation has been delivered in many different ways. Each new method has increased speed but also brought new concerns.

Horatio Alger

A Harvard graduate at nineteen and the son of a Unitarian minister, Horatio Alger found success as a writer in the 1800s. Beginning in 1868, with *Ragged Dick, or, Street Life in New York,* he authored a series of uplifting novels for children. After that work, he began volunteering at a home for runaway boys. Alger's novels were born from his conversations with many of the home's residents, whose real life challenges became a part of the writer's fiction.

Alger's books sold for ten cents—they were among the first of the dime novels. These inexpensive books were also known as "city stories." As urban areas grew after the Civil War, stories about them became popular. Set in places like New York, Boston, and Philadelphia, his stories made heroes of young boys surviving on crowded and dangerous city streets.

A "Horatio Alger" story was one where the young male hero was born poor, but by working hard and avoiding sinful temptation became rich. Alger himself grew rich as his stories found an audience during the Gilded Age. The formula Alger's stories followed helped make them bestsellers. He wrote some 109 books in his lifetime. They sold over 20 million copies.

Parents hoped their children would learn good behavior by reading Alger's stories. Their offspring delighted in the tales of success. It was a perfect series for the times.

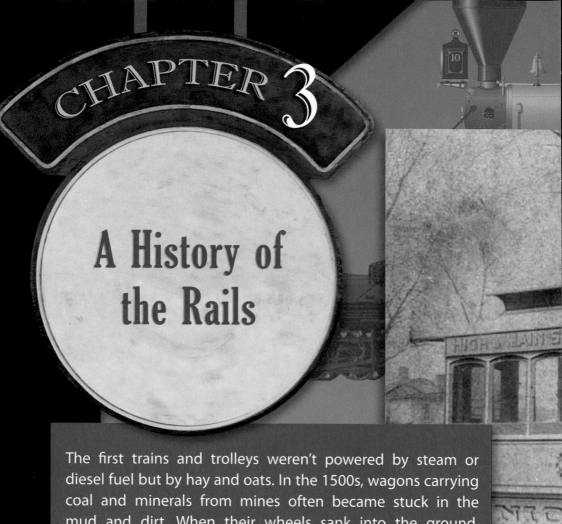

CHAPTER 3

A History of the Rails

The first trains and trolleys weren't powered by steam or diesel fuel but by hay and oats. In the 1500s, wagons carrying coal and minerals from mines often became stuck in the mud and dirt. When their wheels sank into the ground, pulling the load became very difficult. "Wagonways" were created by laying wooden planks along the road and running the carts on top of them.

The English had improved upon this basic design by the 1700s. They carved grooves in the wheels of their carts so the wheels fit snugly on the rails they laid. Iron strips were added to the tops of the wooden rails, which wore out fast from constant use and from the notoriously wet weather of England. In the 1800s, all-iron rails were used on these early railroads.

In the same century, a number of "hay-powered" railroads began running in the United States. The omnibus, a large horse-drawn carriage, provided early public transit, but it

This 1880s photo shows what was called a "horsecar" line on Main Street in Columbus, Ohio. The car was actually pulled by mules.

certainly wasn't rapid transit. Eventually rails were set down, leading to the horsecar, which resembled a carriage more than it did a modern train, as horses or mules pulled the cars along the tracks.

In 1830, the Baltimore and Ohio Railroad (B&O) began operating one of the first trains for commuters. Thirteen miles (twenty-one kilometers) of track ran between Baltimore and the village of Ellicott's Mills for cars hauling passengers and freight. These horse-powered trains were the first in the United States to move people as well as products.

Being pulled by a horse was faster and easier than walking, but not by much. Fortunately eighteenth-century railroads benefited from a seventeenth-century invention: the steam engine. Steam engines relied upon a simple principle understood for hundreds, even thousands of years. When water is heated, it creates steam. When steam is forced into a chamber, it creates pressure. Steam can be used to drive a piston—a solid piece of metal contained inside a tube. Steam causes the piston to move up and down; if a rod is connected to the piston it can accomplish many things, including turning wheels.

Although Thomas Newcomen used a crude steam engine to pump water out of a British coal mine, James Watt perfected the design. Often falsely credited as the inventor of the steam engine, Watt's achievement lay in crafting one that could be widely used. Developed in 1765, Watt's steam engine was used commercially ten years later.

The Industrial Revolution, the period when many workers moved from country farms to factories in the cities, could not have happened without Watt's steam engine. The radical transformation in eighteenth-century America, where for the first time large numbers of people moved hundreds of miles from their birthplace, was powered by the steam locomotive.

In 1804, Richard Trevithick mounted a steam engine on a four-wheeled carriage designed to roll along tracks. Twenty-one years later, the world's first permanent public railroad began operating in England. The Stockton and Darlington Railway carried freight and passengers

The *Best Friend of Charleston* was the pride of the South Carolina Canal and Railroad Company.

using steam locomotives. In 1830, the South Carolina Canal and Railroad Company began the first scheduled steam railroad service for passengers and freight. By 1833, its 136 miles (219 kilometers) of track between Charleston and Hamburg, South Carolina, made it the longest railroad in the world.

Faster and eventually more comfortable than horse-drawn carriages, steam-powered trains exploded in popularity. By 1835, locomotives operated by some 200 different railroad companies traveled along more than 1,000 miles (1,600 kilometers) of track in nine states.

In 1862, President Abraham Lincoln signed the Pacific Railroad Act during the height of the Civil War. Just seven years later, the Central Pacific and Union Pacific railroads met at Promontory Summit in Utah after laying more than 1,700 miles (2,700 kilometers) of track between them. The transcontinental railroad would help bring travelers west, and in its own way made the country a little bit smaller.

Locomotives are usually powered one of three ways. Steam-powered locomotives rely on burning coal or fuel oil to heat water. Although steam engines are still used in a few countries, including China and India, in the United States they are limited to theme parks and museums.

Most commercial locomotives in the United States are diesel-electric. In a diesel-electric locomotive, power from a massive diesel engine is turned into electricity by a generator and then sent to electric motors underneath the locomotive. The electric motors propel the locomotive, which moves the train's cars.

While today people may worry about the pollution produced by diesel engines, a century ago pollution from steam-powered engines was an even greater concern. Smoke from burning coal is very dangerous in confined spaces. Trains traveling through tunnels put anyone in a car with an open window at risk. Unprotected engineers often became quite sick. A few died. It was the quest for a cleaner, safer alternative that led to the third type of locomotive—one powered solely by electricity.

Diesel train in Alaska

A 1930s postcard shows the *Orange Blossom Special* running through orange groves in Florida. Trains like this one used diesel power.

"It looks like a nip and tuck race between the gasoline motor car and the electric locomotive to decide which will do the most to give the steam locomotive the harder push toward the scrap heap," Bernard Meiklejohn explained in his 1907 article "New Motors On Railroads."

"Why are the railroads being electrified?" he asked. Partly "because the public, taught by the trolley lines that it is possible to travel without being forced to breathe smoke and collect cinders, have demanded relief from present railroad conditions and the railroads have been disposed to heed." Meiklejohn said that the thousands of travelers entering and leaving New York City endured a smoke-filled tunnel so horrific one man called it the perfect preparation for hell.[1]

Not long after Richard Trevithick began experimenting with steam-powered locomotives, a Scottish inventor named Robert Davidson was doing the same thing with electricity. In 1837, he powered an electric

locomotive that used batteries. It turned out that his batteries, which couldn't be recharged, cost a lot more than the coal used to power steam locomotives. It took Werner von Siemens's development of an electric generator in the mid-1800s to make electricity cheap enough for railroads to consider this source of alternative power.

Davidson also experimented with an even more advanced system relying upon electromagnets—magnetism created by electricity. Although magnets power the fastest trains in the world today, not only was Davidson's magnetic train never used by a railroad, it was smashed to pieces by steam mechanics who were afraid it would take away their jobs.

In Lichterfelde, Germany, the first commercial electric street railway began operating in 1881. In the United States in 1887, electric locomotives were used to pull hundred-car freight trains along three miles (five kilometers) of dedicated track in Pennsylvania. Less than a

In 1881, the world's first electrically powered commuter trolley—the Gross-Lichterfelde Tramway—began operating in Lichterfelde, a suburb of Berlin, Germany.

decade later, Baltimore, Maryland, boasted the first use of electricity to pull regular freight. Operated by the B&O, electric locomotives pulled trains through its Howard Street Tunnel, which was 1.4 miles (2.3 kilometers) long. The electric locomotives got their power from an electric rail running along one side of the tunnel's ceiling. They pulled the entire train, including the steam locomotive. It was the first mainline railroad electrification in the United States.

In 1888, American inventor Frank Sprague began running the Richmond Union Passenger Railway in Richmond, Virginia. It was the first large electric railway in the United States.

One "electrified" rail line advertised its advantages, promising riders of "The St. Paul Road across the Great Continental Divide, vision unobscured by smoke and luxurious travel unimpeded by cinders or fumes."[2] Across Europe most locomotives used after the early 1900s were electric powered. In the United States, locomotives relied on steam well into the twentieth century. Electricity was mainly used to propel streetcars and trolleys within cities.

The adoption of electric trains was driven by the risk of steam engines in long tunnels, like the Howard Street Tunnel in Baltimore. By 1890, steam locomotives were banned in the London underground line. Instead, electric trains traveled beneath the city's streets. In New York, it took a tragedy to promote widespread use of electric trains.

"By the turn of the twentieth century, hundreds of steam locomotives arrived at Grand Central Station daily, at a rate of one every forty-five seconds," according to "The American Experience," a PBS program. "The Park Avenue Tunnel, built to remove trains from Manhattan's surface and boost public safety, was itself dangerous: dark, smoky, with poor visibility. On January 8, 1902, an express train from White Plains missed signals and plowed into the back of a commuter train that was backed up at the tunnel. Fifteen people were killed instantly and dozens more were bloodied and burned. It was the worst train accident in New York City history."[3]

Grand Central Station shown with the Park Avenue Tunnel below

PARK AVE. TUNNEL

Following the Park Avenue Tunnel tragedy, electrically powered trains were required in most of Manhattan (a borough of New York City). On the other side of the country, electric trains and trolleys transformed the small, dusty community of Los Angeles into the sprawling megacity we know today.

Grand Central Terminal

"No stairways—instead there are ramps," boasted one description of New York City's Grand Central Terminal. It went on to explain, "Stairways are not only a nuisance, but dangerous when traversed by large crowds. . . . There is room in the concourses and waiting rooms for 30,000 people at one time without crowding."[4]

For nearly ten years, the former Grand Central Depot was rebuilt. The depot opened in 1871, and the reconstruction lasted from 1903 to 1911. Over $200 million was spent on a station that would feature forty-six tracks with suburban electric trains traveling into the lower level and mainline trains to the top level. The rail yard had an average depth of thirty feet (nine meters) below street level.

Despite the construction, trains continued running. Up to 1912, a temporary station was used at Lexington Avenue and 43rd Street. Opening at one minute past midnight on February 2, 1913, the Grand Central Terminal—generally called Grand Central Station—featured Beaux-Arts architecture. That style originated in France during the 1800s, and its grand scale was perfect for the Gilded Age building with a main concourse that was more than 125 feet (38 meters) high. The station at 42nd Street and Park Avenue soon became an anchor for some of the most expensive real estate in the world. Today, 750,000 people pass through the station every day. The number rises to more than a million during major holidays.

CHAPTER 4

City Life

"From the mountain tops to the seashore, from the coastline to the desert's edge, the electric way is prepared for your comfort, pleasure and convenience,"[1] a guide to the early twentieth-century Pacific Electric Railway promised. Offering speed and safety as well, the trolley system carried passengers across the rapidly expanding city of Los Angeles.

Workers used it to get to jobs, families rode it on the weekends, and children took it to school. Nearly everyone had the chance to step onboard a trolley from downtown to Pasadena or from hot inland desert towns like San Bernardino to the beach communities of Santa Monica and Newport. The trolleys helped make possible the enormous size of modern-day Southern California. Yet when the first streetcars arrived in the 1870s, the city's population was counted in the thousands, not in the millions. Public transit was powered by horses, just as it was in Baltimore fifty years earlier.

Early Los Angeles and the electric train system

To the north, San Francisco's famous cable cars began when a local resident named Andrew Smith Hallidie patented them in 1871. The cars gripped onto a huge loop of cable that ran in a slot between the tracks. The cable was moved by steam engines in the powerhouse. An operator used a lever to stop and start the car. After being adopted in San Francisco in 1873, the cars quickly replaced many horse-drawn streetcars. Perfect for that hilly and compact city, they were less than ideal for a spread-out city like Los Angeles.

In 1874, Judge Robert M. Widney, an early founder of the University of Southern California, helped launch the first streetcar line in Los Angeles. Tracks were laid for over two miles (three kilometers) from the Mission District to Sixth Street. For ten cents, early commuters had an easier way to travel downtown. The system's popularity led to more horse-drawn streetcars and tracks along the streets of Orange, Riverside, and San Bernardino counties. Steam-powered locomotives fueled the city's growth when major railroads added Los Angeles stops, but it took electric-powered streetcars to expand its dimensions until it approached the size it is today.

The streetcars that altered Los Angeles were inspired in London. Visiting the city, Frank Sprague was troubled by the foul smoke filling the city's tunnels. Returning to the United States he soon improved on a design by his boss, inventor Thomas Edison.

Edison had debuted his alternative to steam engines—an electrically powered locomotive—in 1880. Its speed of forty miles (sixty-four kilometers) per hour terrified the people willing to ride it. The inventor decided he wasn't interested in developing it commercially.

In 1883, Sprague joined Edison's company, but he left the next year. As the head of Sprague Electric Railway and Motor Company, he was unable to convince railroads to convert their steam engines to electricity. Shifting his focus, he began developing streetcars. In 1887, he was hired to electrify a street railway in Richmond, Virginia. He completed installation the next year.

Although the first trolleys in Los Angeles, California, were actually "horse powered," the first electric streetcar system began operating in 1887.

Covering twelve miles (nineteen kilometers), the system handled forty cars. Two years later, across the country more than 200 electric street railways were either being built or were already operational. Half of them used Sprague-manufactured equipment. Many more used his designs.

These cars could go up steep hills impossible for steam engines. They were clean and fast. Because of the efficient way electric power could be delivered (or cut off), electric trains could exit stations quickly and come to a stop faster than steam engines.

The first trolley to be electrified in Los Angeles ran along Pico Street. Although it began operating in 1887, an entire line would not be electrified for several years.

In 1895, Moses Sherman and his brother-in-law Eli Clark opened the first interurban, or "between cities," electric streetcar system. It ran between Pasadena and Los Angeles. The next year, tracks crossed the future cities of Beverly Hills, Hollywood, and Santa Monica. By 1889, they could no longer afford to run the lines they had built. Henry Huntington and his uncle Collis (who was president of the Southern Pacific Railroad) took over.

For more than fifty years, Henry Huntington's electric streetcar system, the Pacific Electric Railway, served Southern California communities. At its peak, its trolleys ran on 1,164 miles (1,873 kilometers) of track linking more than fifty communities in the counties of Los Angeles, San Bernardino, Riverside, and Orange. The bright red cars became famous (although there were also green, olive, and yellow cars in the system). Operating from 1895 to 1961, the system "could honestly boast that it was the largest and most efficient urban system in the world,"[2] claims author Spencer Crump in his book *Ride the Big Red Cars.*

One Pacific Electric advertisement asked potential riders why they should "waste time waiting for steam trains when you can take a car from any cross street every fifteen minutes?"[3] The interurban trolleys were not limited to Los Angeles. They were adopted across the United States as the best, fastest way to move people.

By 1920, electric interurban systems would employ more than 100,000 people across the country and would be the fifth largest industry. There would be double-decker trolleys and open trolleys called "Breezers" because they were open to cool breezes. Some trolley companies even built amusement parks along their lines as a way of making extra money.

The electric trolley's development did not just make commutes within urban areas faster and safer. Many believed the electric trolleys adopted in Southern California were responsible for the area's sprawl. Today, many people live sixty miles (ninety-five kilometers) or more from where they work and often spend three hours a day commuting.

"Electric streetcars and interurbans allowed sprawl in cities such as Los Angeles, a process that would be further encouraged by the automobile. Many city street patterns owe their existence to electric streetcar routes,"[4] says Derek Hayes in his book *Historical Atlas of the North American Railroad.*

The electric train was crucial to the rise of cities in America for they enabled people to live farther away from their jobs, and each other. Soon, however, electric streetcars did not reduce traffic. Instead, in cities across the country, they created it.

Leo Daft

A major improvement in electrical power came from an English electrical engineer. Leo Daft's father was friends with Werner von Siemens. Growing up, Leo soon shared the older man's interest in electricity. Raised in Birmingham, England, Daft believed the best opportunities for inventors were in the United States.

In his forties, Daft moved from England and set up a successful photo studio in Troy, New York. After his father's death, Daft began an electrical company in 1879. He constructed machinery powered by electricity and also built electric power plants in Massachusetts and New York.

Leo Daft

Four years after opening his company, Daft began experimenting with electric locomotives. After being hired by the Saratoga, Mt. McGregor, and Lake George Railroad, he constructed an electric locomotive he called the *Ampere.* By 1885, the Daft Electric Company had installed the first commercially operated electric railroad in the United States. The system built for the Baltimore Union Passenger Railway would be used in a number of cities, including New York City, where it was used on the elevated railroad.

Although his first streetcar was powered by an electrified third rail, this wasn't safe where roads crossed the tracks. Daft worried about someone getting hurt by accidentally stepping on the electrified third rail. He worked on a means of delivering electricity by a wire that would be suspended overhead. A jointed framework called a pantograph would deliver electricity to the train. Since tracks for trolleys are often level with the street, eliminating the third rail design was a big reason trolleys became popular.

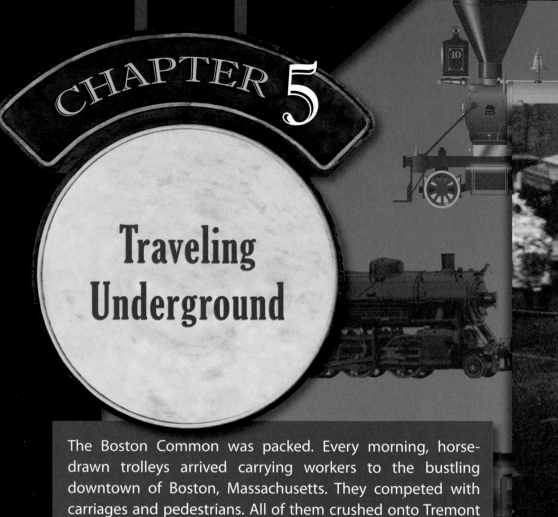

CHAPTER 5

Traveling Underground

The Boston Common was packed. Every morning, horse-drawn trolleys arrived carrying workers to the bustling downtown of Boston, Massachusetts. They competed with carriages and pedestrians. All of them crushed onto Tremont Street, which ran alongside the Common. Every night, the same vehicles carried departing workers. In between, delivery vehicles kept the area nearly immobilized.

By the 1890s, the trolleys were powered by electricity, not horses. Yet this advancement only seemed to increase the number of people flooding into the city every day, which added to the traffic. In 1895, some 400 electric trolleys jammed into Tremont Street alone. There was no more room on the roads. Boston officials decided it was time to go under them.

Speeding along inside a vehicle dozens of feet below ground, underneath office buildings and apartment houses and even big rivers is not a futuristic fantasy. For over a century, it has been reality for many city dwellers.

Boston's Union Station in the 1890s

Unlike trolleys and buses, which must compete with passenger cars, trains can travel above or below most roads. Today, a typical passenger train holds as many as 1,500 commuters. And unlike steam engines, electrically powered trains can spend their entire journey below ground.

Building tunnels for trains to travel below ground was hardly a new concept when Boston officials began to ponder a subway. Proposed in the 1840s, tunneling was adopted in London using modified steam engines in 1863. By 1890, the trains traveling through London's "Tube" were electrified. Still, it had never been attempted in the United States.

One of the more challenging sections for the proposed subway would be the tunnel running beneath Boston Harbor. As risky as building a tunnel under dry land can be, doing so under a big body of water is even more dangerous. Here again, England led the way.

Attempting to build tunnels had tragic and predictable outcomes. Collapsing walls and ceilings injured or killed workers. Then one day, engineer Marc Isambard Brunel found inspiration from a shipworm. This saltwater clam is sometimes called the "termite of the sea."

Burrowing through wood, the tiny shipworm faces some of the same challenges as people tunneling beneath a city. The shipworm protects its head with shells on either side. It releases a substance behind it that hardens and maintains the tiny creature's tunnel.

Brunel's tunneling shield offered similar protections for subway workers. Instead of a shell, he designed thirty-six compartments. Inside each compartment, tunnelers would remove a single oak plank, dig out less than five inches of dirt, and then move the shield forward. At the end of the shield, workers would remove discarded dirt before shoring up the walls with bricks.

Begun in 1825, the tunnel beneath London's Thames River took eighteen years to complete. Despite the precautions, many workers lost their lives working beneath the surface. Yet when it was completed, it represented a huge step forward. It was significant enough to inspire another dreamer.

Workers tunneling under the Thames River used Brunel's shield to dig out dirt behind oak planks. Once all of the workers in all of the compartments had dug out the dirt behind the planks, powerful jacks pushed the shield forward.

Charles Pearson began planning an underground train for London in 1843. Building the tunnel was less of an obstacle than what traveled through it. Fumes from steam engines had to be vented out of the tunnel. Ventilation shafts were built, including one in a rich neighborhood that was disguised to look like the front of a house.

By the time Boston voters approved subway construction in 1894 by a 15,483 to 14,212 vote, electricity was the standard power for subway trains. While commuters would no longer have to risk breathing in deadly smoke from a steam engine, there was a concern that most people still wouldn't consider riding on a subway. In the late nineteenth century, the idea of riding a train underground was frightening to many people. After all, some people thought, the dead were buried underground and it was where their spirits lingered.

Those fears seemed justified when workers reached the edge of the Old Common Burial Ground. Expecting to relocate just a few bodies, they instead found over nine hundred unmarked graves and their corpses. Knowledge about germs was fairly new in the 1890s. Many

New York City's subway system may be better known, but Boston's underground electric train was the first in the United States. Seen here is the Tremont Street Tunnel, which passenger trains began using on September 1, 1897.

people feared that the bodies had contaminated the soil, and subway riders were bound to get sick.

If worrying about angry spirits wasn't enough for some, while Boston's subway was being built, it made traffic conditions even worse. Just as highway construction slows traffic, when work began on the subway, numerous commuters and local businesses were affected. Using a common technique called "cut and cover" meant digging large trenches across streets and parks. Paths were blocked, and familiar streets were rerouted. Utilities had to be relocated. Steam-powered cranes helped move loads of concrete used to build the walls and floor while the roof was brick.

Transit Commission Chairman George Crocker dug the first ceremonial shovelful of dirt on March 28, 1895. The Tremont Street tunnel opened for passengers on September 1, 1897. The second phase relied on an elevated railway, or an "El," which was far easier to construct. Running on tracks built above the street instead of under it, "El" trains

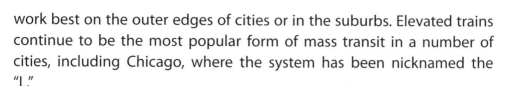
work best on the outer edges of cities or in the suburbs. Elevated trains continue to be the most popular form of mass transit in a number of cities, including Chicago, where the system has been nicknamed the "L."

"Chicago is a classic example of railroad-fueled growth; railroads extended the city's influence far to the west, but a network of shorter lines also allowed its workers to reach the downtown head offices to work. Today such lines, in Chicago and elsewhere, could not be replaced by roads of any sort and still have remotely the same capacity,"[1] explains author Derek Hayes.

Boston's elevated portion was completed on June 10, 1901. The tunnel beneath Boston Harbor was completed on July 4, 1903, when workers from opposite ends of the harbor met in the middle. Boston had the United States' first subway system and the first tunnel of its kind to go under water. New York City's better-known (and longer) subway system would not even begin construction until 1904.

Both the New York and Boston systems were immediately popular. Riders evidently feared traffic more than they did sharing space with the dead. Traffic, at least in the beginning, subsided. Today subway systems like Boston's "T" (for the Massachusetts Bay Transit Authority) are one of the fastest, most popular forms of city transportation. Subways have even been adopted in Los Angeles, where fears of earthquakes collapsing tunnels did not prevent the completion of a transit system that carries riders far beneath the city's streets.

In 1920, passenger rail travel reached an all-time high, with 1.2 million passengers boarding 9,000 intercity trains and racking up 47 million passenger miles a day. In the following decade, passenger rail traffic began to lose its prominent position with the widespread use of the automobile. The introduction of diesel powered streamliners in the 1930s brought a renewed interest in train travel, but the railroad's share of intercity trips continued to decline prior to World War II.

The Red Cars of Los Angeles gave way to cars. Henry Ford's assembly line produced automobiles that were reliable and inexpensive. For the

A replica of a Red Car

first time, the average person could afford a car to drive from home to work and back. Given the choice between sharing space with a stranger on a public train or driving in a car alone or with friends and family, most chose the car. In 1918, one in thirteen families owned a car, but by 1929, four out of five families owned one—the number of cars on the road jumped from 8 million to 23 million in that time.

Today efforts to increase the use of public transit from buses to light rail and mainline trains has had mixed results. In densely populated cities like New York, where people mainly live close together in apartment buildings, public transit is used by many residents, regardless of income. "Intercity passenger rail works best on short-to-medium-distance high volume routes," explains Hayes, "which is why it works so well in Europe. The Northeast coast of the United States has similar population densities, and so such rail links work there also."[2]

In cities that are spread out like Los Angeles, convincing people to travel by rail or bus remains a challenge. Although ridership has been growing, less than ten percent of the city's workers use public transit to get to their jobs.

"The problem was the automobile that eventually sentenced the electric interurban [trolley] to death. The automobile itself was not the real villain in the interurban story: this role was played by the roads and highways demanded for the growing number of private vehicles,"[3] explains Spencer Crump in *Ride the Big Red Cars*. Yet for many, the dream of electric trains and trolleys for modern travel has not ended.

Fast Trains to Somewhere

Bullet trains

Looking across the ocean to Europe and Asia, many in the United States wonder why there are no "bullet trains" in this country. Electric-powered trains in France have reached speeds over 300 mph (480 km/h). Fast, efficient electric trains in Europe and Asia are generally funded by government, because building the necessary electric lines and then maintaining them is too costly for most businesses. In order to make money running an electric train, a private company would have to charge many times what is charged in European countries. This is because their governments subsidize the trains—they pay a portion of each fare with money from other sources, usually taxes.

In the United States, the Acela Express is one of the few divisions of Amtrak to make money. Created by the U.S. government in 1971, Amtrak has taken over intercity service in the United States. Begun in 1996, it was delayed because miles of catenary line—the overhead wires that supply electrical power—had to be modified for its expected high speeds of 150 mph (240 km/h). The train began operations in December 2000.

Despite the train's ability to reach high speeds, on much of its Boston, Massachusetts, to Washington, D.C., route it averages 86 mph (138 km/h). With stops in a number of cities including New York, Philadelphia, and Baltimore, the train successfully services the most densely populated region in the United States.

In 2008, voters in California—a large state with a more spread-out population—voted to approve financing for a high-speed train traveling from Southern California to San Francisco. Budgeted at just over $30 billion when the vote took place, four years later estimates have placed the cost of the train at nearly $100 billion dollars. Construction has not begun.

1830 The first section of the Baltimore and Ohio Railroad opens for business, making it the first common carrier in the United States.

1862 President Abraham Lincoln signs the Pacific Railway Act, authorizing construction of the nation's first transcontinental railroad.

1863 London becomes the first city in the world to have a subway; the underground trains are powered by steam locomotives.

1869 Train tracks laid by the Central Pacific and Union Pacific railroads meet at Promontory Summit in Utah, completing construction of the first transcontinental railroad.

1886 Henry Ford builds his first automobile

1887 An electric locomotive pulls a hundred-ton freight train three miles (five kilometers) through Pennsylvania's Lykens Valley.

1893 Southern California's first interurban line is opened when the Pasadena and Los Angeles Electric Railway Company begins running between the two cities. In San Diego, cable cars are converted to electric power.

1895 In Baltimore, Maryland, the ban on steam engines within the Howard Street Tunnel leads to the country's first mainline electrification.

1901 Henry Huntington buys the Pasadena and Los Angeles Electric Railway, incorporating it as the Pacific Electric Railway.

1903 Steam engines are prohibited south of Harlem in the New York City borough of Manhattan.

1905 A Chicago to New York electric line is proposed that would let travelers make the trip in ten hours, but the project proves too expensive.

1911 Henry Huntington sells the Pacific Electric Railway to the Southern Pacific Railroad; by this time, it is one of the largest interurban systems in the country.

1913 West Virginia's Elkhorn Tunnel, bored in 1888, is electrified along its 3,000 feet (900 meters).

1913 The Oakland, Antioch, and Eastern Railway, which travels from Oakland to Sacramento, is extended to Chico; it runs for 185 miles (300 kilometers), making it is the longest electric interurban line in North America until it closes in 1945.

1920s The Pacific Electric manages more than 1,000 miles (1,600 kilometers) of track and 2,700 trains daily including a short subway in downtown Los Angeles, until the end of the decade, when buses begin to replace trolleys.

Chapter 1. The Difficult Journey
1. Spencer Crump, *Ride the Big Red Cars: How Trolleys Helped Build Southern California* (Corona Del Mar, CA: Trans-Anglo Books, 1970), p. 15.

Chapter 2. The Gilded Age
1. Les Standiford, *Last Train to Paradise: Henry Flagler and the Spectacular Rise and Fall of the Railroad that Crossed an Ocean* (New York: Crown Publishers, 2002), p. 48.
2. Mark Twain and Charles Dudley Warner, *The Gilded Age* [1873] (New York: Penguin, 2001), p. 59.
3. Henry Allen, *What it Felt Like: Living in the American Century* (New York: Pantheon Books, 2000), p. 23.
4. Charles W. Calhoun, *The Gilded Age: Perspectives on the Origins of Modern America* (Wilmington, DE: Scholarly Resources, 1996), p. 31.
5. Thomas J. Schlereth, *Victorian America: Transformations in Everyday Life, 1876–1915* (New York: HarperCollins Publishers, 1991), pp. 95–96.

Chapter 3. A History of the Rails
1. Bernard Meiklejohn, "New Motors on Railroads Electric and Gasoline Cars Replacing the Steam Locomotive," *The World's Work, Volume 13* (New York: Doubleday, Page & Co., 1900–1932), and online at http://books.google.com/books?id=3lfNAAAA MAAJ&pg=PA8446#v=onepage&q&f=false, pp. 8446–8447.
2. Derek Hayes, *Historical Atlas of the North American Railroad* (Berkeley, CA: University of California Press, 2010), p. 145.
3. Public Broadcasting Service, "Park Avenue Tunnel Crash, 1902," American Experience, January 19, 2012, http://www.pbs.org/wgbh/americanexperience/features/primary-resources/grandcentral-parkave/
2. Derek Hayes, *Historical Atlas of the North American Railroad* (Berkeley, CA: University of California Press, 2010), p. 145.
4. Derek Hayes, *Historical Atlas of the North American Railroad* (Berkeley, CA: University of California Press, 2010), p. 159.

Chapter 4. City Life
1. "Official Transportation and City Map of Los Angeles, Cal. and Suburbs," housed in the Special Collections of the Charles E. Young Research Library at the University of California Los Angeles, and online at http://content.cdlib.org/ark:/13030/hb7f59p4 06/?order=2&brand=calisphere
2. Spencer Crump, *Ride the Big Red Cars: How Trolleys Helped Build Southern California* (Corona Del Mar, CA: Trans-Anglo Books, 1970), p. 5.
3. Ibid., p. 61.
4. Derek Hayes, *Historical Atlas of the North American Railroad* (Berkeley, CA: University of California Press, 2010), p. 141.

Chapter 5. Traveling Underground
1. Derek Hayes, *Historical Atlas of the North American Railroad* (Berkeley, CA: University of California Press, 2010), p. 202.
2. Ibid., p. 201.
3. Spencer Crump, *Ride the Big Red Cars: How Trolleys Helped Build Southern California* (Corona Del Mar, CA: Trans-Anglo Books, 1970), p. 158.

Allen, Henry. *What it Felt Like: Living in the American Century.* New York: Pantheon Books, 2000).

Calhoun, Charles W. *The Gilded Age: Perspectives on the Origins of Modern America.* Wilmington, DE: Scholarly Resources, 1996.

Crump, Spencer. *Ride the Big Red Cars: How Trolleys Helped Build Southern California.* Corona Del Mar, CA: Trans-Anglo Books, 1970.

Grand Central Terminal, "History: Restored, Rejuvenated, Rededicated," http://www.grandcentralterminal.com/info/restored.cfm

Hayes, Derek. *Historical Atlas of the North American Railroad.* Berkeley, CA: University of California Press, 2010.

"Horatio Alger," http://www-sul.stanford.edu/depts/dp/pennies/1860_alger.html

Houk, Randy. *"Railroad History: Important Milestones in English and American Railway Development,"* Pacific Southwest Railway Museum Association, Inc., http://www.sdrm.org/history/timeline/

Lears, T. J. Jackson. Rebirth of a Nation: The Making of Modern America, 1877–1920. New York: HarperCollins, 2009.

"Mark Twain: Biography," The Official Web Site of Mark Twain, http://www.cmgww.com/historic/twain/about/bio.htm

Public Broadcasting Service, "Park Avenue Tunnel Crash, 1902," *American Experience,* January 19, 2012, http://www.pbs.org/wgbh/americanexperience/features/primary-resources/grandcentral-parkave/

"The Red Cars of Los Angeles," http://www.usc.edu/libraries/archives/la/historic/redcars/

"Red Cars: The Pacific Electric Collection," Orange Empire Railway Museum, " http://www.oerm.org/pages/pe.html

Schlereth, Thomas J. *Victorian America: Transformations in Everyday Life, 1876–1915.* New York: HarperCollins Publishers, 1991.

Standiford, Les. *Last Train to Paradise: Henry Flagler and the Spectacular Rise and Fall of the Railroad that Crossed an Ocean.* New York: Crown Publishers, 2002.

Titone, Nora. *My Thoughts be Bloody.* New York: Free Press, 2010

World of Invention, "Generator," http://www.bookrags.com/research/generator-woi/>

Books

Brimmer, Larry Dane. *Subway: The Story of Tunnels, Tubes, and Tracks*. Honesdale, PA: Boyd Mills Press, 2004.

Hewett, Joan. *Tunnels, Tracks, and Trains: Building a Subway*. New York: Lodestar Books, Dutton, 1995.

Hynson, Colin. *A History of Railroads*. Milwaukee, WI: Gareth Stevens Publishing, 2006.

McKendry, Joe. *Beneath the Streets of Boston: Building America's first Subway*. Boston: David R. Godine, 2005.

Weitzman, David. *A Subway for New York*. New York: Farrar, Straus and Giroux, 2005.

On the Internet

Let's Rediscover the Locomotive Together

    http://www.locomotives-and-trains.com/

Orange Empire Railway Museum

    http://www.oerm.org/

Orange Empire Railway Museum Snapshots of Pacific Electric Railway Trolley Cars

    http://www.youtube.com/watch?v=sun58cBvNMo&feature=player_embedded

"Red Cars: The Pacific Electric Collection

    http://www.oerm.org/pages/pe.html

San Diego's Early Streetcars

    http://www.sandiegohistory.org/collections/streetcar/streetcar.htm

The Trolley Stop

    http://www.trolleystop.com/index.htm

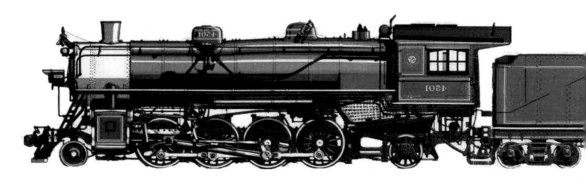

commercial (kuh-MUHR-shul)—Engaging in work or trade designed to earn money.

commuter (kuh-MEW-tor)—Someone who travels regularly from home to work and back.

commuter rail—A regional railway propelled by electricity or diesel for passenger train service between cities and towns or suburbs.

conductor (kuhn-DUCK-tor)—The person who collects the fares on a trolley or train.

engineer (en-juh-NEER)—A person who designs and builds engines, machines, or public works. On a train, the engineer is the driver.

heavy rail—An electric railway system that handles a high volume of traffic on high-speed passenger trains that run along separate rights-of-way from which all other traffic is banned.

isthmus (ISS-mess)—A narrow strip of land with sea on either side.

light rail—An electric railway system that can operate single or multiple cars in subways, on exclusive rights-of-way, or on streets, and discharge passengers at station platforms or street level; they are normally powered by overhead wires. They have a "light" volume of traffic compared to heavy rail systems.

locomotive (LO-kuh-mo-tiv)—A self-propelled vehicle for pushing or pulling freight or passenger trains.

pantograph (PAN-tuh-graf)—The jointed framework that delivers electricity from an electrified wire to a train's propulsion system.

suburb (SUH-burb)—A smaller community within commuting distance of a city.

ABOUT THE AUTHOR

Born in Boston, Massachusetts, John Bankston began writing articles while still a teenager. Since then, over two hundred of his articles have been published in magazines and newspapers across the country, including travel articles in *The Tallahassee Democrat, The Orlando Sentinel* and *The Tallahassean*. He is the author of over sixty biographies for young adults, including works on Alexander the Great, scientist Stephen Hawking, author F. Scott Fitzgerald and actor Jodi Foster. At thirteen he took his first solo train trip, traveling from Boston to Richmond, Virginia, to visit relatives. Since then he has enjoyed numerous rail adventures including trips in Italy, a cross-country trip from San Diego, California, to Brattleboro, Vermont, and a trip from Los Angeles, California, to Portland, Oregon. He lives in Newport Beach, California.